Ethical ITSM

Navigating

Data Privacy, AI and Integrity

in IT Services

Naza Semenoff

CONTENTS

Preface

Navigating the Ethical Landscape in IT Service Management

Welcome to "Ethical ITSM: Navigating Data Privacy, AI, and Integrity in IT Services." If you are reading this, chances are you're either an IT professional, an IT service manager, or just someone who enjoys a good read about ethics (yes, those people do exist!). Whatever your reason, I'm thrilled you're here.

Let's be honest: ethics in IT Service Management (ITSM) might not sound like the most exciting topic at first glance. You might think it's all about rules, regulations, and a lot of "don't do this" and "don't do that." But here's the thing—I'm here to tell you that ethics in ITSM is actually a lot like life itself: full of challenges, decisions, and yes, the occasional "oops" moment. And like life, it's best navigated with a sense of humor and a good cup of coffee (or tea, if that's your thing).

In the rapidly evolving world of Information Technology Service Management (ITSM), the importance of ethics has never been more pronounced. We're constantly navigating a landscape where technological advancements, customer expectations, and regulatory requirements intersect. It's a bit like trying to juggle flaming swords while riding a unicycle—you've got to keep your balance, or things can go south really fast.

But let's not get too serious too quickly! The idea behind this book isn't just to hammer home the importance of ethics in ITSM but to explore it in a way that's both informative and, dare I say, enjoyable. I mean, if we can't have a little fun while discussing data privacy and AI biases, what are we even doing here?

This book was born out of the recognition that while the technical and process-oriented aspects of ITSM are often discussed, the ethical dimensions receive comparatively less attention. Yet, these ethical considerations are integral to the responsible management and delivery of IT services. They influence how we handle data privacy, the way we implement artificial intelligence (AI), and our approach to managing IT services with integrity and accountability.

Now, I know what you're thinking—"Wow, ethics sounds heavy." And sure, it can be. But it's also the stuff that makes our jobs meaningful. It's what turns a routine IT decision into something more, something that impacts real people in real ways. And trust me, nothing keeps you awake at night quite like the thought of accidentally breaching GDPR. (If you're new to that acronym, don't worry—we'll get into it. Just know it's the kind of thing that can make or break your day, or your budget.)

The objective of this book is twofold. Firstly, it aims to shine a light on the ethical challenges inherent in modern ITSM practices, particularly focusing on areas like data privacy, the ethical use of AI, and the overarching need for integrity in managing IT services. Secondly, it seeks to provide practical guidance and frameworks to help ITSM professionals navigate these ethical dilemmas. Through a combination of theoretical insights, real-world case studies, and a sprinkle of humor, this book endeavors to equip ITSM practitioners, managers, and decision-makers with the knowledge and tools to uphold ethical standards in their work.

Our target audience is broad, encompassing anyone involved in the ITSM sector. This includes IT service managers, CIOs, IT professionals, consultants, and students of ITSM. Whether you are a seasoned ITSM expert or new to the field, this book offers valuable perspectives on integrating ethical considerations into your ITSM practices. Plus, if you've ever had a nightmare about explaining a data breach to a client, this book might just become your new best friend.

As we delve into the chapters that follow, I invite you to reflect on the ethical dimensions of your work in ITSM. In doing so, we hope to foster a deeper understanding of how ethical considerations are not just peripheral concerns but are central to the effective, responsible, and sustainable management of IT services. And who knows? Maybe we'll have a few laughs along the way.

So, grab your favorite drink, find a comfortable spot, and let's embark on this journey together. Because in "Ethical ITSM," we're not just exploring the ethical landscape—we're doing it with a smile, a bit of wit, and a lot of heart. Together, we'll navigate the challenges, embrace best practices, and strive towards a future where ethics and ITSM go hand in hand, shaping a more responsible and trustworthy IT industry.

Let's dive in!

Chapter 1

Introduction to Ethics in ITSM

Ethics in IT: Because just turning it off and on again doesn't solve

everything.

What is ITSM?

Before diving into the ethical aspects, let's clarify what ITSM actually is—because let's face it, if you're going to spend your time reading about it, you should at least know what it is!

Imagine the IT department in any organization as the unsung hero—the one that keeps everything running smoothly, fixes problems when things go wrong, and, most importantly, ensures that your computer doesn't crash right before that crucial presentation. Now, take that idea and apply it on a grand scale. That's ITSM.

At its core, ITSM is all about managing and delivering IT services to meet the needs of an organization. It's like being the conductor of a very complex orchestra, where each musician (or IT service) needs to play their part perfectly to create harmony. ITSM isn't just about fixing things when they break (although that's certainly a part of it); it's about proactively managing IT in a way that aligns with the organization's goals.

Defining Ethics in ITSM

Ethics in ITSM refers to the principles and standards that govern the conduct of IT professionals and organizations in the delivery and management of IT services. It encompasses a wide range of practices, from how personal data is handled to the fairness and transparency of AI algorithms used in service management. Ethics in ITSM is about making decisions that are not only effective but also morally sound and socially responsible.

Ethical considerations in ITSM touch upon various aspects, including but not limited to, data privacy, security, compliance with laws and regulations, and the equitable treatment of clients and employees. The goal is to ensure that IT services are managed and delivered in a way that respects individual rights, promotes trust, and aligns with societal values.

Expert Opinion: The Growing Role of Ethics in ITSM Dr. Luciano Floridi, Professor of Philosophy and Ethics of Information at the University of Oxford, is a leading authority on the ethical implications of digital technologies. He emphasizes that "Ethics is not an optional add-on to IT governance; it is a core aspect that must be integrated into every decision and practice. As digital technologies become more pervasive, the ethical responsibilities of IT professionals are magnified."

Dr. Floridi's insights underscore the importance of developing a robust ethical framework that guides the use of technologies like AI, big data, and cloud services, ensuring they benefit society as a whole and do not exacerbate existing inequalities.

Historical Perspective: Evolution of Ethical Considerations in ITSM

The history of ethics in ITSM is closely tied to the evolution of information technology itself. In the early days of computing, ethical concerns were primarily focused on issues like software piracy and the accuracy of data. However, as technology advanced and became more integrated into everyday life, the scope of ethical considerations in ITSM expanded significantly.

The advent of the internet and digital data storage brought data privacy and security to the forefront. Issues such as hacking, identity theft, and unauthorized data access became major concerns. The introduction of regulations like the General Data Protection Regulation (GDPR) marked a significant step in addressing these concerns, setting a new standard for data protection and privacy.

Historical Timeline of Ethics in ITSM

- **1960s-1970s:** Early ethical issues focused on software piracy and data accuracy.
- **1980s-1990s:** With the rise of personal computing and the internet, data privacy and security became more prominent concerns.
- **2000s:** The proliferation of digital data and online services led to increased focus on identity theft, hacking, and unauthorized data access.

- **2010s:** The introduction of GDPR and other regulations emphasized the importance of data protection and privacy, setting new standards for ITSM practices.

- **2020s:** The rise of AI and machine learning introduced new ethical challenges, such as bias in algorithms and the impact of automation on employment.

As AI and machine learning become more embedded in ITSM, fresh ethical concerns have surfaced. Issues such as bias in AI systems, the transparency of AI-driven outcomes, and the influence of automation on workforce dynamics are now essential considerations for ITSM professionals.

The Need for Ethical ITSM: Why Ethics Matter in Today's IT Landscape

In the current digital era, where technology permeates almost every aspect of our lives, the importance of ethics in ITSM cannot be overstated. Ethical ITSM practices are crucial for several reasons:

1. **Building Trust:** In an age where data breaches and misuse of personal information are common, ethical practices in ITSM

help build trust with customers and stakeholders. Trust is a fundamental component of any successful IT service.

2. **Compliance and Legal Obligations:** With the increasing number of regulations governing data protection and privacy, ethical ITSM practices are essential for compliance and avoiding legal repercussions.

3. **Social Responsibility:** ITSM professionals have a responsibility to ensure that their practices do not harm individuals or society. This includes being mindful of privacy, avoiding bias in AI, and ensuring accessibility and fairness in service delivery.

4. **Sustainable Business Practices:** Ethical practices in ITSM contribute to the long-term sustainability of an organization. Unethical practices, while they may provide short-term gains, can lead to significant reputational and financial damage in the long run.

5. **Adapting to Emerging Technologies:** As new technologies emerge, they bring new ethical challenges. ITSM professionals must be prepared to continually adapt their ethical frameworks to ensure the responsible use of these technologies.

Case Study: Navigating Ethical Dilemmas in ITSM

In 2017, a multinational financial services company, which we'll call FinTechCorp, found itself in the midst of an ethical crisis that tested its ITSM practices and commitment to ethics.

The Situation: FinTechCorp has recently rolled out a major software update to its customer management system. This update was designed to enhance the user experience by integrating new AI-driven features that could predict customer needs and offer tailored services. The update had gone through extensive testing, but as is often the case in the complex world of IT, not everything went as planned.

Shortly after the update was deployed, the ITSM team discovered a serious issue: a vulnerability in the system allowed unauthorized access to sensitive customer data, including financial records and personal information. The flaw had the potential to expose the data of millions of customers across multiple countries.

The Dilemma: The discovery put FinTechCorp in a difficult position. The ITSM team was faced with an ethical dilemma that had no easy answers. On one hand, they could immediately inform their customers and the public about the data breach, in line with transparency and ethical standards. However, doing so would likely cause panic, damage the company's reputation, and lead to a significant loss of business.

On the other hand, the company could quietly work to fix the issue before it was exploited or became widely known, potentially avoiding immediate backlash. This approach, however, would mean withholding critical information from customers whose data was at risk—a decision that could be seen as deceptive and unethical.

The Decision: After intense discussions among the ITSM team, legal advisors, and senior management, FinTechCorp decided to prioritize transparency and customer trust over short-term reputational damage. The company chose to go public with the information, notifying affected customers immediately and offering comprehensive support, including credit monitoring services and personal consultations to mitigate potential risks.

To ensure the issue was resolved swiftly, the ITSM team worked around the clock to patch the vulnerability and conducted a thorough review of the entire system to prevent similar issues in the future. They also collaborated with cybersecurity experts to reinforce their data protection measures.

The Outcome: While the decision to go public led to a temporary dip in FinTechCorp's stock prices and a wave of negative media coverage, the long-term effects were more positive. Customers appreciated the company's honesty and proactive approach, which helped rebuild trust and loyalty. The transparent handling of the situation even attracted new customers who valued ethical business practices.

Moreover, the case became a turning point for FinTechCorp's ITSM strategy. The company introduced more rigorous testing protocols, enhanced its AI ethics guidelines, and implemented a new framework for handling data-related incidents with greater transparency and accountability. This experience also served as a valuable lesson in the importance of integrating ethics into every aspect of ITSM, from decision-making to crisis management.

Lessons Learned:

1. **Transparency Builds Trust:** Even in the face of potential backlash, being open and honest with customers can strengthen trust and improve long-term relationships.

2. **Ethical Decision-Making:** Prioritizing ethical principles, even when it's difficult, can lead to more sustainable and positive outcomes for the business and its stakeholders.

3. **Proactive Measures:** Ensuring robust testing, continuous monitoring, and strong cybersecurity measures are critical in preventing and responding to ethical dilemmas in ITSM.

4. **Responsibility and Accountability:** A culture of accountability, where ethical decisions are supported by senior leadership, is essential for navigating crises effectively.

By choosing the path of integrity, FinTechCorp not only resolved the crisis but also positioned itself as a leader in ethical ITSM practices, setting a standard for others in the industry.

Conclusion: The Dynamic Nature of Ethics in ITSM

Ethics in ITSM is a dynamic and essential field that requires ongoing attention and commitment. As technology continues to evolve, so must our approach to ethical challenges in IT service management. The discussion in this chapter sets the stage for a deeper exploration of specific ethical issues in ITSM, including data privacy, the use of AI, and the overall integrity of IT services.

So, as we delve further into the ethical landscape of ITSM, remember that while the tools and technologies may change, the principles of fairness, transparency, and responsibility remain constant. And who knows? With a little bit of humor and a lot of integrity, navigating the ethical challenges of ITSM might just become one of the most rewarding parts of the job.

Chapter 2

Data Privacy and Protection in ITSM

Data privacy: It's like wearing pants—essential for keeping your

assets covered.

Understanding Data Privacy in ITSM

Data is often referred to as the new gold—it's incredibly valuable, sought after, and must be carefully protected. In the context of ITSM, data privacy is about ensuring that personal and sensitive information is handled in a way that protects individuals' rights and maintains their trust. This responsibility falls squarely on the shoulders of ITSM professionals, who must balance the needs of the organization with the privacy rights of users.

Imagine data privacy as the lock on the vault where all this digital gold is stored. Your job in ITSM is to ensure that this vault is secure, that only authorized people have the key, and that the lock is checked and updated regularly to guard against any would-be thieves.

The Importance of Data Privacy in ITSM

In ITSM, data privacy isn't just a technical concern—it's a critical ethical issue. Protecting user data isn't just about avoiding legal trouble; it's about respecting the privacy of individuals and maintaining the trust that is essential for any successful IT service. Let's be real: if customers can't trust you with their data, they're not going to trust you with anything else, either.

Data privacy in ITSM involves a wide range of practices, including securing data against unauthorized access, ensuring data is only used for its intended purpose, and providing users with control over their own information. It's about making sure that the systems and processes in place not only comply with regulations like GDPR but also align with broader ethical standards.

The Balancing Act: Security vs. Privacy

One of the biggest challenges in ITSM is finding the right balance between security and privacy. On one hand, you need to secure data to protect it from breaches, hackers, and all the other digital villains lurking out there. On the other hand, you need to respect individuals' privacy, ensuring that their data isn't being used or accessed in ways they haven't agreed to.

Think of it like being a bouncer at an exclusive club. You want to keep out the troublemakers, but you also don't want to infringe on the privacy of the guests who are there to have a good time. In ITSM, this balancing act involves implementing security measures that are strong enough to protect data without being so invasive that they compromise privacy.

The GDPR Impact: A Game-Changer for Data Privacy

The General Data Protection Regulation (GDPR), which came into effect in 2018, has been a game-changer for data privacy. It set a new standard for how organizations must handle personal data, with hefty fines for those who fail to comply. But GDPR is more than just a set of rules to follow; it's a reflection of growing concerns about how personal data is managed in the digital age.

Under GDPR, individuals have more control over their data than ever before. They have the right to know what data is being collected, how it's being used, and to request its deletion if they so choose. For ITSM professionals, this means implementing processes that are transparent, compliant, and respectful of these rights. Compliance isn't just about avoiding fines; it's about doing the right thing for your customers and the broader society.

Case Study: The GDPR Impact In 2018, when GDPR was implemented, many organizations were caught unprepared for the stringent requirements. One notable example is a global tech company, which we'll call TechGlobal, that faced a significant challenge with GDPR compliance. Unaware of the depth of GDPR's reach, TechGlobal initially underestimated the complexity of achieving full compliance.

Shortly after GDPR came into effect, TechGlobal was fined €50 million for failing to comply with transparency and consent requirements related to its data collection practices. The fine was a wake-up call for the company, prompting a comprehensive overhaul of its data privacy policies and practices.

TechGlobal's ITSM team had to act quickly to address the shortcomings. They implemented new processes for obtaining explicit user consent, improved data encryption methods, and established a dedicated data protection officer role to oversee compliance efforts. The company also invested in extensive staff training to ensure that everyone—from developers to customer service reps—understood the importance of GDPR compliance.

While the fine was a significant financial hit, the changes that TechGlobal implemented helped restore customer trust and positioned the company as a leader in data privacy. The case highlights the importance of being proactive in data privacy efforts and the consequences of failing to meet regulatory requirements.

Global Comparison of Data Privacy Laws

While GDPR is a major player in the world of data privacy, it's not the only game in town. Around the globe, different regions have their own laws and regulations that govern how data should be handled. And just like how different countries drive on different sides of the road, these laws can vary significantly.

- **CCPA (California):** On the west coast of the United States, the California Consumer Privacy Act (CCPA) gives residents the right to know what personal data is being collected and to opt out of the sale of their data. It's like GDPR's laid-back cousin, focused on consumer rights with a sunny Californian twist.

- **PDPA (Singapore):** Over in Singapore, the Personal Data Protection Act (PDPA) emphasizes accountability and consent, with a bit more flexibility in how data can be used. Think of it as a more practical approach, allowing businesses to innovate while still protecting personal data.

- **LGPD (Brazil):** Meanwhile, in Brazil, the Lei Geral de Proteção de Dados (LGPD) brings its own flair to data protection. Similar to GDPR, it includes provisions for data portability and specific rights for children's data. It's like a tropical blend of GDPR with a focus on inclusivity and accessibility.

For ITSM professionals, navigating these different regulations can feel like a world tour of data privacy—without the jet lag. The key is to stay informed, be adaptable, and ensure that your data management practices are compliant with the laws in all the regions where you operate.

Practical Tips for Enhancing Data Privacy in ITSM

Now that we've covered why data privacy is so important, let's talk about some practical steps you can take to enhance data privacy within your ITSM practices:

1. **Conduct Regular Audits:** Just like how you wouldn't let your car go without a regular check-up, your data management practices need regular audits to ensure everything is running smoothly and compliantly.

2. **Implement Encryption:** Encryption is like putting your data in a safe. Even if someone tries to break in, they won't be able to access the contents without the key. Make sure sensitive data is encrypted both at rest and in transit.

3. **Train Your Team:** Data privacy isn't just the responsibility of the IT department. Everyone in your organization should be aware of best practices for handling data. Regular training sessions can help keep data privacy top of mind.

4. **Use Privacy by Design:** When developing new IT services or systems, consider data privacy from the outset. This means building in privacy features from the ground up, rather than tacking them on as an afterthought.

5. **Stay Informed:** Data privacy laws and regulations are constantly evolving. Make sure you're staying up to date with the latest developments so you can adapt your practices accordingly.

Conclusion: Protecting Data, Protecting Trust

In the world of ITSM, data privacy isn't just a nice-to-have—it's a must-have. It's the foundation of trust between your organization and the people whose data you manage. By prioritizing data privacy, you're not just avoiding legal trouble; you're building a reputation as a trustworthy and responsible organization.

So, the next time you're handling data, think of it as handling gold—valuable, precious, and deserving of the highest level of care. Because in the end, protecting data is about protecting trust, and that's something worth safeguarding.

Chapter 3

Ethical Use of AI in ITSM

AI: It's like having a really smart assistant, but make sure it doesn't get too smart for its own good—or yours.

The Rise of AI in ITSM

Artificial Intelligence is no longer just a concept from science fiction; it's here, and it's transforming the way we manage IT services. From automating routine tasks to predicting issues before they happen, AI is becoming an integral part of ITSM. But as with any powerful tool, AI in ITSM comes with significant ethical considerations.

AI in ITSM can handle a wide range of applications, such as chatbots that manage customer inquiries, algorithms that predict when a server might go down, and tools that automatically categorize and prioritize incidents. These advancements are making ITSM more efficient and effective, allowing IT professionals to focus on more strategic tasks.

However, as AI takes on more responsibilities, the ethical considerations become increasingly complex.

Why Ethics Matter in AI for ITSM When it comes to AI, ethics isn't just a buzzword—it's a critical component of responsible implementation. Think of AI as a really smart, slightly overenthusiastic assistant. It's eager to help, but without proper guidance, it might end up making decisions that have unintended consequences.

For example, AI algorithms are only as good as the data they're trained on. If that data is biased, the AI's decisions will be too. This could lead to unfair outcomes, such as certain groups of users receiving lower levels of service or being unfairly targeted by automated processes. And let's be honest, nobody wants to be the company that accidentally creates a robot overlord with a chip on its shoulder.

Ethics in AI for ITSM is about ensuring that the technology is used in a way that is fair, transparent, and accountable. It's about making sure that AI serves the needs of all users, not just the ones who fit neatly into an algorithm's preconceived notions. And most importantly, it's about maintaining human oversight—because while AI can do a lot, some decisions should always be made by a person.

Ethical Frameworks for AI in ITSM

To navigate the ethical challenges of AI, it's important to have a framework in place. Here are a few key principles to keep in mind when implementing AI in ITSM:

1. **Human Agency:** AI should support human decision-making, not replace it. This means that AI should be used to provide insights and recommendations, but the final decision should always rest with a human. After all, nobody wants to be told, "The algorithm made me do it."

2. **Fairness:** AI systems should be designed to treat all users fairly. This means ensuring that the data used to train AI is diverse and representative, and that the AI's decisions do not discriminate against any group. Think of it as the golden rule for robots: treat others—and their data—as you would want to be treated.

3. **Transparency:** AI processes should be transparent and understandable. Users should be able to see how decisions are made and have the ability to challenge or question those decisions if necessary. It's like being able to look under the hood of your car—except instead of an engine, you're looking at a

complex algorithm that decides whether your IT ticket gets resolved today or next week.

4. **Accountability:** There must be clear lines of accountability for decisions made by AI systems. If something goes wrong, there should be a human who can step in and take responsibility. After all, you can't exactly take an algorithm to court—yet.

Case Study: The Double-Edged Sword of AI Automation

AI automation in ITSM is a bit like a double-edged sword. On one hand, it can significantly increase efficiency, reduce human error, and free up IT staff to focus on more strategic tasks. On the other hand, it can also lead to job displacement, create new risks, and even exacerbate existing inequalities if not implemented carefully.

Consider the case of GlobalTech, a large multinational corporation that decided to implement AI-driven automation to streamline its IT service desk operations. The AI system was designed to automatically categorize and prioritize incoming support tickets, allowing the IT team to focus on high-priority issues.

However, shortly after deployment, the IT team noticed a troubling pattern. The AI system, which had been trained on historical data, was consistently deprioritizing tickets from certain departments, particularly those involving non-technical staff. Upon investigation, it was discovered that the training data reflected a historical bias in the organization, where non-technical issues were often given lower priority.

This bias had been unknowingly embedded into the AI's decision-making process, leading to unfair treatment of certain employees. GlobalTech faced a difficult decision: should they pull the AI system and revert to manual processes, or should they try to retrain the AI to eliminate the bias?

The company chose the latter, dedicating significant resources to retrain the AI system with a more balanced dataset and implementing strict oversight mechanisms to ensure fairness in ticket prioritization. They also introduced a feedback loop, allowing employees to flag issues with the AI's decisions, which further helped in refining the system.

The experience taught GlobalTech valuable lessons about the importance of fairness, transparency, and human oversight in AI implementation. The AI system, once retrained, delivered significant efficiency gains without compromising fairness or trust.

The Future of AI in ITSM: Opportunities and Challenges

As AI continues to evolve, its role in ITSM is only going to grow. In the future, we can expect to see even more sophisticated AI systems that can predict issues before they occur, optimize IT service delivery in real-time, and even manage entire IT infrastructures autonomously.

But with these opportunities come new challenges. As AI takes on more complex tasks, ethical considerations will become even more critical. Organizations will need to stay vigilant, ensuring that their AI systems are aligned with ethical principles and that they continue to prioritize human oversight.

In the end, the future of AI in ITSM is bright—but only if we approach it with a clear sense of responsibility. By keeping ethics at the forefront, we can ensure that AI serves as a force for good in IT service management, helping organizations deliver better, more efficient services while maintaining the trust and confidence of their users.

Conclusion: Embracing AI with a Human Touch

AI has the potential to revolutionize ITSM, making it faster, smarter, and more efficient. But like any powerful tool, it must be used with care. By embracing AI with a human touch—ensuring that it is fair, transparent, and accountable—we can harness its power while avoiding its pitfalls.

So, the next time you're implementing an AI system in your ITSM processes, remember: with great power comes great responsibility. And while AI might be the superhero of ITSM, every superhero needs a good sidekick to keep them in check—and that's where you come in.

Chapter 4

Managing IT Services with Integrity

Integrity in ITSM: Like duct tape for your moral compass—keeps everything in place, even under pressure.

What Does Integrity Mean in ITSM?

Integrity is one of those words that gets tossed around a lot, but what does it really mean in the context of IT Service Management (ITSM)? Simply put, integrity in ITSM is about doing the right thing, even when no one is watching—or, more realistically, when everyone is watching, especially during an IT crisis.

In the world of ITSM, integrity means being honest, transparent, and accountable in every action you take. It's about ensuring that your IT services are delivered in a way that is not only efficient and effective but also fair and just. Whether you're managing a critical incident, implementing a new system, or simply responding to a routine ticket, integrity should be at the core of your decision-making process.

Think of integrity as the foundation of a house. Without it, everything else—no matter how well-designed or technologically advanced—can come crashing down. In ITSM, integrity is what ensures that your services are reliable, your processes are fair, and your team is trusted by the entire organization.

The Importance of Integrity in ITSM

So why is integrity so important in ITSM? Well, for starters, IT services are often the backbone of an organization's operations. If the IT department loses integrity, the entire organization can suffer. Imagine a scenario where an IT service manager decides to cut corners on a security update to meet a deadline. It might seem like a minor decision at the time, but if that shortcut leads to a data breach, the consequences could be catastrophic.

Integrity in ITSM is also about trust. Users rely on IT services to do their jobs, and they trust that those services will be available, secure, and reliable. If that trust is broken—whether through a lack of transparency, a failure to communicate, or an unethical decision—it can be incredibly difficult to rebuild. And let's be honest, once trust is lost, it's a bit like trying to put toothpaste back in the tube—messy, frustrating, and not entirely successful.

Finally, integrity in ITSM is about setting the right example. IT professionals are often seen as the guardians of an organization's most critical assets: its data, its systems, and its intellectual property. By acting with integrity, IT leaders can set a standard for the rest of the organization, demonstrating the importance of ethical decision-making and accountability.

Common Ethical Dilemmas in ITSM

Ethical dilemmas are a dime a dozen in ITSM, and they often pop up when you least expect them. Here are a few common scenarios you might encounter—and some tips on how to navigate them with your ethical compass intact:

1. **Cutting Corners vs. Meeting Deadlines:** Imagine you're managing a critical system upgrade, and the deadline is looming. You know that cutting a few corners could help you meet the deadline, but it might compromise the system's security. What do you do? The answer, of course, is to resist the temptation to

cut corners. Integrity means prioritizing long-term security over short-term gains—even if it means a few sleepless nights.

2. **Transparency vs. Confidentiality:** You've just discovered a major security vulnerability in a system used by the entire company. Do you inform all the users immediately, or do you keep it under wraps until you've fixed the issue? This is a tough one, but integrity means being transparent, even when it's uncomfortable. While it's important to maintain confidentiality where necessary, users have a right to know about risks that could affect them.

3. **Accountability vs. Blame-Shifting:** A mistake has been made, and it's causing a significant disruption. Do you take responsibility, or do you point the finger at someone else? Integrity means owning up to your mistakes and working to fix them, rather than shifting the blame. After all, nobody likes a blame game—unless it's followed by cake.

Building a Culture of Integrity in ITSM

Creating a culture of integrity in ITSM doesn't happen overnight, but it's well worth the effort. Here are some practical steps you can take to foster a culture where integrity is valued and practiced by everyone on the team:

1. **Lead by Example:** As an IT leader, your actions set the tone for the rest of the team. By consistently acting with integrity—whether in decision-making, communication, or conflict resolution—you show your team that ethical behavior is non-negotiable.

2. **Establish Clear Ethical Guidelines:** Make sure your team knows what's expected of them when it comes to ethical behavior. This could be through a formal code of conduct, regular training sessions, or even just open discussions about what integrity looks like in practice. It's like the "golden rule" of ITSM: treat others—and their data—the way you'd want to be treated.

3. **Encourage Transparency:** Foster an environment where transparency is the norm, not the exception. This means being open about challenges, mistakes, and decisions. When your team sees that transparency is valued, they're more likely to act with integrity themselves.

4. **Reward Ethical Behavior:** Recognize and reward team members who demonstrate integrity, whether through formal recognition programs or just a simple "thank you." When people see that ethical behavior is appreciated, they're more likely to make it a priority.

5. **Hold Everyone Accountable:** Ensure that everyone on the team is held to the same standards of integrity. This means addressing unethical behavior when it occurs and ensuring that there are consequences for actions that undermine trust and accountability.

Case Study: Integrity in Action

In a large healthcare organization, the CIO was tasked with overseeing the implementation of a new patient data management system. During testing, the IT team discovered a significant security flaw that could potentially expose sensitive patient data. Despite pressure from the board to meet the project deadline due to financial incentives, the CIO decided to delay the launch to fix the security issue. This decision, although costly in the short term, reinforced the organization's commitment to patient safety and data integrity.

Here's how the scenario unfolded:

The Dilemma: The board was pushing hard for the project to go live as scheduled. Delaying the launch would mean missing key performance indicators (KPIs) tied to bonuses and investor expectations. The IT team, aware of the security flaw, knew that launching the system as is could put patient data at serious risk.

The Decision: The CIO had to make a tough call: prioritize financial and reputational gains by meeting the deadline, or uphold the organization's ethical commitment to patient safety. The CIO chose integrity over immediate gains, opting to delay the project and fix the security flaw before the system went live.

The Outcome: While the delay initially caused frustration among stakeholders, the decision ultimately proved to be the right one. The secure launch of the system not only protected patient data but also enhanced the organization's reputation for putting ethics and safety first. In the long run, this decision bolstered trust among patients, employees, and investors alike.

Lessons Learned: The case illustrates that acting with integrity, even when it's difficult, can lead to more sustainable outcomes. By prioritizing ethical considerations, the CIO not only protected sensitive data but also reinforced the organization's values and long-term success.

The Role of Ethical Audits in ITSM

One way to ensure that integrity is maintained in ITSM is through regular ethical audits. Unlike traditional audits, which focus on compliance and financial performance, ethical audits assess whether an organization's practices align with its values and ethical standards.

An ethical audit in ITSM might involve reviewing how data is handled, ensuring that privacy policies are being followed, and evaluating whether the organization's IT services are being delivered in a way that is fair and transparent. It's a bit like having a moral compass for your IT department—making sure you're staying on the right path.

Conclusion: Integrity as the Backbone of ITSM

In IT Service Management, integrity isn't just a nice-to-have—it's a must-have. It's what ensures that your IT services are reliable, your processes are fair, and your team is trusted by the entire organization.

By acting with integrity in every aspect of ITSM, you're not only doing the right thing—you're also building a foundation for long-term success.

So, the next time you're faced with a tough decision in ITSM, remember: integrity is the best policy. Whether it's resisting the urge to cut corners, being transparent about challenges, or taking responsibility for mistakes, acting with integrity will always lead to better outcomes. And who knows? You might even inspire others in your organization to do the same.

Chapter 5

Ethical Decision-Making in ITSM

Making ethical decisions in ITSM: Because flipping a coin isn't how you should decide who gets admin rights.

Why Ethical Decision-Making Matters in ITSM

Let's face it: decision-making in ITSM isn't always straightforward. It's not like choosing between coffee or tea (although, let's be honest, in the USA or France, it's usually coffee—but not necessarily if you're in Japan, where a good green tea might be your go-to). In ITSM, the decisions you make can have far-reaching consequences—not just for your systems and services, but for your users, your organization, and even society at large.

Ethical decision-making in ITSM is about navigating the complex landscape of technical requirements, business goals, and human values. It's about making choices that are not only effective and efficient but also fair, responsible, and aligned with the ethical standards of your organization. And yes, it's about avoiding those "uh-oh" moments when you realize that a seemingly minor decision has led to a major ethical dilemma.

Think of ethical decision-making as the GPS for your ITSM journey. It helps you stay on course, avoid roadblocks, and reach your destination without ending up in a ditch—or worse, in the news for all the wrong reasons.

The Ethical Decision-Making Process

Making ethical decisions in ITSM doesn't have to be a guessing game. By following a structured process, you can ensure that your decisions are well-considered, transparent, and justifiable. Here's a step-by-step guide to ethical decision-making in ITSM:

1. **Identify the Ethical Issue:** The first step is to recognize that an ethical issue exists. This might seem obvious, but in the fast-paced world of ITSM, it's easy to overlook the ethical implications of a decision. Ask yourself: Is there a potential conflict of interest? Could this decision impact users' rights or

privacy? Are there any stakeholders who might be affected by this choice?

2. **Gather Information:** Once you've identified the ethical issue, gather all the relevant information. This includes technical details, business requirements, and the perspectives of all stakeholders. The more information you have, the better equipped you'll be to make an informed decision. It's like trying to solve a puzzle—you need all the pieces to see the full picture.

3. **Consider the Alternatives:** Before jumping to a conclusion, consider all the possible alternatives. What are the potential outcomes of each option? How do they align with your organization's ethical standards? What are the risks and benefits? This is the time to think creatively and explore all the possibilities.

4. **Evaluate the Options:** Now that you have a list of alternatives, it's time to evaluate them. Use ethical frameworks to assess each option. Here are some of the most commonly used ethical frameworks in ITSM:

   o **Utilitarianism:** This framework focuses on the outcome of decisions and advocates for actions that maximize overall happiness or benefit. In ITSM, this might mean choosing the option that delivers the greatest good for the greatest number of users, even if it requires some sacrifices.

- **Deontological Ethics:** Rooted in the idea that certain actions are inherently right or wrong, this framework emphasizes adherence to rules, duties, or obligations. In ITSM, this could involve sticking to privacy policies or regulatory requirements, regardless of the potential outcomes.

- **Virtue Ethics:** This framework emphasizes the importance of moral character and virtues such as honesty, integrity, and fairness. In ITSM, this might mean making decisions that reflect the organization's core values, even if they involve difficult trade-offs.

- **Rights-Based Ethics:** This approach centers on respecting and protecting the fundamental rights of individuals, such as privacy, freedom of expression, and autonomy. In ITSM, this could mean prioritizing user consent and transparency in data handling.

- **Care Ethics:** Focused on relationships and the needs of others, this framework emphasizes empathy, compassion, and care. In ITSM, this might involve making decisions that prioritize the well-being of users and employees, even when it's not the most efficient option.

This step is crucial for ensuring that your decision is not only practical but also morally sound.

5. **Make the Decision:** After careful consideration, it's time to make your decision. Choose the option that best aligns with your ethical principles and organizational values. And remember, in ITSM, sometimes the "right" decision isn't the easiest or the most popular one—but it's the one that will stand the test of time.

6. **Implement the Decision:** Once you've made your decision, put it into action. Communicate the decision clearly to all stakeholders and be prepared to explain your reasoning. Transparency is key to maintaining trust and credibility.

7. **Review the Decision:** After implementing your decision, take the time to review the outcomes. Did the decision achieve the desired results? Were there any unintended consequences? What lessons can be learned for the future? This step is all about continuous improvement—because in ITSM, there's always room for growth.

Common Ethical Dilemmas in ITSM Decision-Making

Ethical dilemmas are a dime a dozen in ITSM, and they often pop up when you least expect them. Here are a few common scenarios you might encounter—and some tips on how to navigate them with your ethical compass intact:

1. **User Privacy vs. Security:** Imagine you're tasked with implementing a new monitoring system to enhance security. The system can track user activity in real-time, but it also raises concerns about privacy. Do you prioritize security at the expense of privacy, or do you find a way to protect both? The ethical approach here is to strike a balance—implementing security measures that are effective but also respect users' privacy rights.

2. **Cost Savings vs. Quality of Service:** Your organization is under pressure to cut costs, and you're considering outsourcing a key IT service to a third-party provider. The cost savings are significant, but there's a risk that the quality of service could suffer. Do you go for the cheaper option, or do you invest in maintaining high-quality service? In this case, integrity means putting users' needs first and ensuring that any cost-cutting measures don't compromise service quality.

3. **Transparency vs. Confidentiality:** You've discovered a potential vulnerability in a critical system, but you're not sure whether to disclose it to the wider organization. On one hand, transparency is important for maintaining trust; on the other hand, you don't want to cause unnecessary panic. The ethical decision here involves being transparent about the risks while also taking steps to mitigate them before they become a bigger issue.

Interactive Ethical Scenarios: Put Yourself in the Hot Seat

Let's put theory into practice with some interactive ethical scenarios. These are designed to help you think through complex ethical dilemmas and make decisions that reflect your organization's values.

Scenario 1: The Overzealous AI You're responsible for deploying a new AI-driven helpdesk system that can automatically categorize and prioritize tickets. The AI is great—almost too great. It's starting to make decisions that could affect users in unexpected ways, such as deprioritizing certain types of requests based on incomplete data. Do you trust the AI's efficiency, or do you step in to ensure that the system is fair and transparent?

- **Option A:** Let the AI do its thing—it's faster and more efficient, and it's learning as it goes.
- **Option B:** Pause the AI's automated decisions and review its processes to ensure fairness and accuracy.

Scenario 2: The Data Breach Dilemma Your organization has experienced a minor data breach. The breach was contained quickly, and the data exposed was not particularly sensitive. Do you inform all affected users immediately, or do you keep it quiet to avoid causing unnecessary alarm?

- **Option A:** Inform all users immediately—transparency is key, even if it causes some short-term panic.

- **Option B:** Keep it quiet and monitor the situation closely, informing users only if the risk escalates.

Scenario 3: The Budget Crunch You're managing a project with a tight budget, and you've just realized that you're going to run out of funds before the project is complete. You have the option to cut corners on quality to stay within budget, or you can request additional funding to ensure the project meets all standards. What do you do?

- **Option A:** Cut corners where possible - getting the project done on time and within budget is the priority.

- **Option B:** Request additional funding—quality should never be compromised, even if it means going over budget.

Building an Ethical Decision-Making Culture

Creating a culture where ethical decision-making is the norm requires effort and commitment. Here are some strategies to help you build a strong ethical foundation in your ITSM team:

1. **Encourage Open Dialogue:** Make it easy for team members to discuss ethical dilemmas and seek advice. Create a safe space where people can voice their concerns and explore different perspectives without fear of judgment.

2. **Provide Ethical Training:** Regular training sessions on ethical decision-making can help reinforce the importance of ethics in ITSM. Use real-world examples and case studies to make the training relevant and engaging.

3. **Lead by Example:** As a leader, your actions speak louder than words. Demonstrate your commitment to ethical decision-making by consistently making choices that align with your organization's values—and by holding others accountable when they don't.

4. **Celebrate Ethical Decisions:** Recognize and reward team members who make difficult ethical decisions, even when it's

not the easiest or most popular choice. This reinforces the message that ethics matter and that doing the right thing is always valued.

Case Study: Ethical Decision-Making in Action

A large retail company, RetailCorp, faced a significant ethical decision during the rollout of a new online payment system. The ITSM team discovered a potential flaw that could allow unauthorized access to customer payment information under specific conditions. The flaw was unlikely to be exploited, but the risk was there.

The Dilemma: RetailCorp was set to launch the payment system during the holiday shopping season, a critical period for the company's revenue. Delaying the launch to fix the flaw would mean missing out on substantial sales, but launching with the flaw could potentially expose customers to financial risk.

The Decision: The ITSM team, along with senior management, decided to delay the launch and fix the flaw, prioritizing customer safety and trust over immediate profits. They communicated the decision transparently to stakeholders, explaining the reason for the delay and the steps being taken to ensure the system's security.

The Outcome: While the delay resulted in a short-term loss of revenue, the decision to act with integrity ultimately paid off. Customers appreciated the company's honesty and commitment to security, which strengthened their trust in the brand. The ethical decision also helped RetailCorp avoid potential legal and reputational issues that could have arisen from launching a flawed system.

Lessons Learned: This case highlights the importance of making ethical decisions, even when they're tough. By prioritizing long-term trust and security over short-term gains, RetailCorp not only protected its customers but also reinforced its reputation as a trustworthy and responsible organization.

Conclusion: Navigating the Ethical Landscape

Ethical decision-making in ITSM isn't always easy, but it's essential for building trust, maintaining integrity, and delivering high-quality services. By following a structured decision-making process, considering all stakeholders, and staying true to your organization's values, you can navigate the ethical landscape with confidence.

And remember: when in doubt, do the right thing—even if it means taking the road less traveled. Because in ITSM, integrity and ethics aren't just buzzwords—they're the compass that guides you toward long-term success.

Chapter 6:

Sustainability and Social Responsibility in ITSM

Saving the planet one kilowatt at a time—because nobody wants their data center to be the villain in an environmental documentary.

The Growing Importance of Sustainability in ITSM

Sustainability and social responsibility aren't just buzzwords—they're becoming central pillars of how organizations operate, and ITSM is no exception. In today's world, where climate change, resource scarcity, and social equity are front and center, organizations are increasingly expected to do their part in addressing these global challenges. And let's be honest, saving the planet is a lot more appealing than explaining why your data center uses enough energy to power a small town.

In ITSM, sustainability means designing and delivering IT services in a way that minimizes environmental impact while maximizing efficiency. It's about reducing energy consumption, managing resources responsibly, and ensuring that the IT services you provide contribute positively to the environment and society. After all, nobody wants to be the organization that's known for its carbon footprint the size of a dinosaur.

The Triple Bottom Line: People, Planet, Profit

When it comes to sustainability in ITSM, it's all about the triple bottom line—balancing people, planet, and profit. Here's what that means:

1. **People:** This aspect focuses on social responsibility—ensuring that your IT services support the well-being of employees, customers, and the wider community. It's about creating a positive impact on people's lives, whether through fair labor practices, inclusive technology design, or contributing to social causes. In other words, it's about being a good neighbor, not just a good business.

2. **Planet:** The environmental aspect of sustainability is all about reducing your organization's ecological footprint. This includes minimizing energy consumption, reducing e-waste, and adopting green IT practices. Think of it as giving Mother Earth a little TLC—because she's been through a lot, and we've got a responsibility to take care of her.

3. **Profit:** Let's not forget that businesses need to be profitable to survive. But here's the thing: sustainability and profitability aren't mutually exclusive. In fact, sustainable practices often lead to cost savings, innovation, and a stronger brand reputation. It's like finding out that eating vegetables is not only good for you, but it can also taste pretty great with the right recipe.

Green IT: Reducing Environmental Impact

Green IT is at the heart of sustainability in ITSM. It's all about making IT practices more environmentally friendly—from the way you power your data centers to how you dispose of old hardware. Here are some practical steps you can take to embrace Green IT:

1. **Energy-Efficient Data Centers:** Data centers are the lifeblood of IT services, but they're also notorious energy guzzlers. By optimizing energy use—whether through advanced cooling systems, virtualization, or renewable energy sources—you can significantly reduce your carbon footprint. And hey, who wouldn't want to brag about their data center being more energy-efficient than their neighbor's fridge?

2. **Sustainable Software Development:** It's not just about the hardware—software can be sustainable too. By designing software that requires less computational power, you can reduce energy consumption and extend the life of devices. It's like the difference between a gas-guzzling SUV and a hybrid car—both get you from point A to point B, but one does it with a lot less environmental impact.

3. **E-Waste Management:** Let's talk about e-waste—those old computers, phones, and gadgets that are collecting dust in your storage room. Proper e-waste management involves recycling, refurbishing, or donating old hardware instead of sending it to the landfill. It's like having a garage sale for your IT department—one person's obsolete equipment could be another person's treasure.

Social Responsibility in ITSM

Social responsibility in ITSM is about more than just reducing your environmental impact—it's also about making a positive contribution to society. Here are some ways ITSM can support social responsibility:

1. **Inclusive Technology:** Ensure that your IT services are accessible to everyone, regardless of age, ability, or background. This includes designing user interfaces that are easy to navigate, providing support in multiple languages, and ensuring that assistive technologies are available for those who need them. After all, technology should be a bridge, not a barrier.

2. **Fair Labor Practices:** ITSM isn't just about technology—it's about people. Ensure that your IT services are delivered by workers who are treated fairly and ethically. This includes paying fair wages, providing safe working conditions, and supporting workers' rights. It's about treating people with the respect and dignity they deserve—because happy employees make for happy customers.

3. **Community Engagement:** Get involved in your local community by supporting initiatives that align with your organization's values. Whether it's providing IT support to local schools, donating old equipment to non-profits, or participating in sustainability programs, community engagement is a great way to show that your organization cares about more than just the bottom line.

Ethical Frameworks for Sustainability in ITSM

To guide your sustainability efforts in ITSM, it's helpful to have a framework in place. Here are a few ethical frameworks that can inform your sustainability practices:

1. **Environmental Ethics:** This framework emphasizes the intrinsic value of the natural environment and the responsibility humans have to protect it. In ITSM, this could involve prioritizing energy efficiency, reducing waste, and minimizing the environmental impact of your operations.

2. **Corporate Social Responsibility (CSR):** CSR is a business model that helps a company be socially accountable—to itself, its stakeholders, and the public. In ITSM, CSR could involve adopting sustainable business practices, supporting social causes, and ensuring that your operations positively impact society.

3. **The Precautionary Principle:** This principle advises that if an action or policy has the potential to cause harm to the public or the environment, in the absence of scientific consensus, the burden of proof falls on those advocating for the action. In

ITSM, this might mean carefully assessing the environmental impact of new technologies before implementing them.

4. **Sustainable Development:** This framework focuses on meeting the needs of the present without compromising the ability of future generations to meet their own needs. In ITSM, this could involve adopting long-term strategies that balance economic, social, and environmental considerations.

Case Study: A Sustainable ITSM Success Story

Let's take a look at a real-world example of sustainability in action. A global telecommunications company recognized that its data centers were consuming a massive amount of energy, contributing significantly to its carbon footprint. To address this, the company launched a comprehensive Green IT initiative with the following steps:

1. **Energy-Efficient Upgrades:** The company replaced outdated servers with energy-efficient models and implemented virtualization to reduce the number of physical servers required. This resulted in a 30% reduction in energy consumption.

2. **Renewable Energy:** The company partnered with renewable energy providers to power its data centers with wind and solar energy, further reducing its reliance on fossil fuels.

3. **E-Waste Recycling:** The company established an e-waste recycling program, diverting tons of electronic waste from landfills and refurbishing old equipment for donation to schools and non-profits.

4. **Employee Engagement:** The company involved its employees in sustainability efforts, offering incentives for energy-saving ideas and encouraging participation in community sustainability programs.

The Outcome: The company not only reduced its environmental impact but also saw significant cost savings and an enhanced brand reputation. And perhaps most importantly, it demonstrated that sustainability and profitability can go hand in hand.

The Business Case for Sustainability

Sustainability isn't just good for the planet—it's good for business too. Here's why:

1. **Cost Savings:** Green IT practices often lead to cost savings, whether through reduced energy consumption, lower operating costs, or more efficient resource use. It's like switching to LED bulbs—there's an upfront cost, but the long-term savings are worth it.

2. **Innovation:** Embracing sustainability can drive innovation, leading to new products, services, and business models. By thinking creatively about how to reduce your environmental impact, you might just stumble upon the next big thing in ITSM.

3. **Brand Reputation:** Today's consumers and employees are increasingly looking for organizations that align with their values. By committing to sustainability, you can enhance your brand reputation and attract customers, partners, and talent who share your commitment to making a positive impact.

4. **Regulatory Compliance:** Let's not forget that many regions have regulations requiring organizations to reduce their

environmental impact. By adopting sustainable practices now, you'll be ahead of the curve—and you'll avoid the headache of scrambling to comply with new regulations later on.

Practical Tips for Implementing Sustainability in ITSM

Now that we've covered why sustainability is so important, let's talk about some practical steps you can take to make your ITSM practices more sustainable:

1. **Conduct an Environmental Audit:** Start by assessing your current environmental impact. Identify areas where you can reduce energy consumption, minimize waste, and improve efficiency. It's like giving your IT operations a green check-up.

2. **Adopt Energy-Efficient Technologies:** Invest in energy-efficient hardware and software. Consider virtualizing your servers, using cloud-based solutions, and optimizing your data centers to reduce energy use. Think of it as upgrading from a gas-guzzler to a hybrid.

3. **Reduce E-Waste:** Implement a robust e-waste management strategy. This could involve recycling old hardware, donating used equipment, or partnering with a certified e-waste recycler.

Remember, one person's outdated tech could be another's treasure.

4. **Engage Your Team:** Encourage your team to get involved in sustainability efforts. Offer training on sustainable IT practices, create a green IT committee, or incentivize energy-saving ideas. Sustainability isn't just a top-down initiative—it's a team effort.

5. **Monitor and Report:** Track your progress and report on your sustainability initiatives. Use metrics to measure your impact and share your successes with stakeholders. It's like keeping score in a game—except the prize is a healthier planet.

Conclusion: The Future of ITSM is Green

Sustainability and social responsibility aren't just trends—they are the future of IT Service Management. By embracing Green IT practices, supporting social responsibility, and balancing the triple bottom line of people, planet, and profit, you can ensure that your IT services are not only effective and efficient but also aligned with the values of your organization and the needs of the world.

So, the next time you're making a decision in ITSM, ask yourself: How can I make this choice more sustainable? How can I reduce the environmental impact? How can I make a positive contribution to society? Because in the end, sustainability isn't just about doing less harm - it's about doing more good.

Chapter 7

Security and Ethics in ITSM

IT security: Locking the door, but also making sure your users don't

feel like they're in digital Alcatraz.

The Intersection of Security and Ethics in ITSM

In the world of ITSM, security is often seen as the guardian at the gate—standing firm to protect systems, data, and users from threats. But security isn't just about firewalls, encryption, and access controls; it's also deeply intertwined with ethics. After all, with great power (and access to sensitive information) comes great responsibility.

Security in ITSM isn't just about keeping the bad guys out; it's also about making sure the good guys are playing by the rules. This means ensuring that your security measures are not only effective but also ethical. It's about finding the balance between protecting the organization and respecting the rights and privacy of individuals.

Because while it's tempting to implement every possible security measure, it's important to remember that security should never come at the expense of ethics.

The Ethical Dilemmas of IT Security

Security in ITSM is rife with ethical dilemmas. Here are a few common scenarios you might encounter—and some tips on how to navigate them without losing your ethical compass:

1. **Surveillance vs. Privacy:** Imagine you're implementing a new monitoring system that tracks user activity to detect potential security threats. The system can log every keystroke, every website visited, and every file accessed. It's a powerful tool for preventing breaches—but it's also a potential invasion of privacy. Do you prioritize security, or do you respect user privacy? The ethical approach here is to implement monitoring in a way that is transparent, limited to what is necessary, and respectful of users' privacy rights. After all, nobody likes feeling like Big Brother is watching their every move—especially when they're just trying to find that one funny cat video.

2. **Data Retention vs. Deletion:** Your organization stores vast amounts of data, much of it sensitive. Keeping data for longer can help with security audits and investigations, but it also increases the risk of that data being exposed in a breach. Should you hold onto the data just in case, or should you delete it to protect privacy? The ethical answer involves balancing the need for data retention with the principle of data minimization—keeping only what's necessary and securely deleting the rest.

3. **Access Control vs. Convenience:** You're setting up access controls for a new system, and the easiest solution is to give everyone broad access to reduce the number of access requests you'll have to manage. But broad access increases the risk of unauthorized access and potential security breaches. Do you choose convenience, or do you enforce strict access controls? In this case, integrity means prioritizing security over convenience, ensuring that access is granted on a need-to-know basis.

The Role of Compliance in IT Security

Compliance is a big part of IT security, and it often brings with it a host of ethical considerations. Organizations are required to comply with various regulations, such as GDPR, HIPAA, or PCI-DSS, which dictate how data must be protected. But compliance isn't just about ticking boxes—it's about understanding the ethical principles behind these regulations and implementing them in a way that truly protects users.

Here's the thing: compliance and ethics aren't always the same. Just because you are compliant doesn't necessarily mean you are acting ethically. For example, you might comply with data retention laws by keeping user data for the minimum required period, but is it ethical to hold onto data for that long if it's no longer needed? The key is to go beyond compliance and consider the broader ethical implications of your security practices.

Ethical Frameworks for IT Security

To navigate the complex relationship between security and ethics in ITSM, it's helpful to have a framework in place. Here are a few ethical frameworks that can guide your security decisions:

1. **Proportionality Principle:** This principle states that security measures should be proportionate to the risks they are designed to mitigate. In ITSM, this might mean implementing strong security controls for sensitive data while using lighter measures for less critical information.

2. **Transparency Principle:** This principle emphasizes the importance of transparency in security practices. Users should be informed about what data is being collected, how it's being used, and who has access to it. In ITSM, this could involve clear communication about monitoring practices and data usage policies.

3. **Accountability Principle:** This principle holds that organizations should be accountable for their security practices and any breaches that occur. In ITSM, this might mean having clear protocols for reporting and responding to security incidents, as well as regular audits to ensure compliance with ethical standards.

4. **Least Privilege Principle:** This principle advocates for granting users the minimum level of access necessary to perform their tasks. In ITSM, this could mean implementing strict access

controls and regularly reviewing user permissions to ensure they align with current responsibilities.

Case Study: Balancing Security and Ethics

Let's take a look at a real-world example of how one organization navigated the intersection of security and ethics. A financial institution was implementing a new security monitoring system that could track employee activities in real-time, including web browsing, email communications, and file access. The goal was to prevent insider threats and detect potential breaches before they happened.

However, the organization's leadership recognized that this level of surveillance could be seen as invasive and could erode trust among employees. They decided to take an ethical approach to the implementation by doing the following:

1. **Transparency:** The organization communicated openly with employees about the new monitoring system, explaining why it was being implemented and how the data would be used. They made it clear that the system was designed to protect the organization, not to micromanage or invade employees' privacy.

2. **Limited Monitoring:** Instead of logging every activity, the organization limited monitoring to activities that were directly related to security risks, such as access to sensitive financial data or unusual network activity. This approach reduced the potential for privacy invasion while still achieving the security objectives.

3. **Employee Involvement:** The organization involved employees in the decision-making process, seeking their input on how the monitoring system could be implemented in a way that balanced security and privacy. This not only improved the system's design but also increased employee buy-in.

4. **Regular Audits:** To ensure that the monitoring system was being used ethically, the organization conducted regular audits of the data collected. These audits helped to identify any potential misuse of the system and ensured that employees' privacy rights were being respected.

The Outcome: The organization was able to implement a security monitoring system that protected against insider threats while maintaining employee trust and respecting privacy. By taking an ethical approach to security, they not only met their security goals but also strengthened their organizational culture.

The Future of Security and Ethics in ITSM

As technology continues to evolve, the ethical challenges of IT security will only become more complex. AI, machine learning, and advanced analytics are increasingly being used in security systems, raising new questions about bias, accountability, and transparency. At the same time, the rise of remote work and cloud computing is blurring the lines between personal and professional data, creating new ethical dilemmas around privacy and surveillance.

In this rapidly changing landscape, organizations must remain vigilant, continuously adapting their security practices to ensure they remain both effective and ethical. This means staying informed about emerging technologies, understanding the ethical implications of new security tools, and always putting users' rights and well-being at the forefront of decision-making.

Practical Tips for Maintaining Security with Integrity

Now that we've explored the ethical considerations of IT security, here are some practical steps you can take to maintain security with integrity in your ITSM practices:

1. **Implement Strong Access Controls:** Use the principle of least privilege to ensure that users only have access to the information they need to perform their roles. Regularly review and update access permissions to prevent unauthorized access.

2. **Conduct Regular Security Audits:** Regular audits can help identify potential vulnerabilities and ensure that security measures are being applied consistently. Use these audits to review both technical and ethical aspects of your security practices.

3. **Provide Transparency to Users:** Clearly communicate your organization's security policies and practices to users. This includes explaining what data is collected, how it is used, and what measures are in place to protect it.

4. **Train Your Team:** Ensure that your IT team is trained in both the technical and ethical aspects of security. Regular training sessions can help reinforce the importance of maintaining security with integrity.

5. **Stay Informed About Emerging Threats:** Security threats are constantly evolving, so it's important to stay informed about the latest developments. Monitor industry news, attend security

conferences, and participate in professional networks to keep your knowledge up to date.

Conclusion: Security with Integrity

In ITSM, security isn't just about protecting data—it's about protecting trust. By approaching security with integrity, organizations can ensure that their security practices are not only effective but also ethical. This means balancing the need for protection with the need for privacy, going beyond compliance to consider the broader ethical implications of security decisions, and creating a culture where ethics and security go hand in hand.

So, the next time you're faced with a security decision in ITSM, remember: security and ethics are two sides of the same coin. Protecting your organization and respecting your users' rights are both essential—and with a little creativity and a lot of integrity, you can achieve both.

Chapter 8

The Future of Ethical ITSM

The future of ITSM is like a sci-fi movie—full of robots, AI, and ethical dilemmas that make your head spin. But hey, at least it's never boring!

Looking Ahead: The Evolving Landscape of ITSM

The future of ITSM is like a high-speed train hurtling toward us—packed with new technologies, emerging trends, and, of course, a whole new set of ethical challenges. As we move forward, the importance of maintaining ethical standards in ITSM will only grow, shaping how organizations design, deliver, and manage their IT services.

In this chapter, we'll explore some of the key trends that are set to transform ITSM, the ethical considerations they bring, and how organizations can navigate these changes with integrity. So, fasten your seatbelts and keep your ethical compass handy—we're heading into the future of ITSM.

The Rise of AI and Automation

Artificial Intelligence and automation are already making waves in ITSM, but we're just scratching the surface of their potential. In the future, AI could take on even more complex tasks, from predictive analytics that preemptively resolve issues before they occur to fully automated service management processes that require minimal human intervention. Sounds like a dream come true, right? Well, not so fast.

While AI and automation offer incredible benefits—efficiency, scalability, and cost savings, to name a few—they also come with significant ethical considerations. For example:

1. **Bias and Fairness:** AI algorithms are only as good as the data they're trained on. If that data is biased, the AI's decisions will be too. This could lead to unfair treatment of certain groups or individuals, especially if the AI is used to make decisions that impact people's lives, such as allocating resources or prioritizing support requests.

2. **Accountability:** As AI takes on more decision-making power, the question of accountability becomes more pressing. If an AI system makes a mistake—or worse, causes harm—who is

responsible? The developer? The IT team? The organization as a whole? These are questions that organizations will need to address as AI becomes more integrated into ITSM.

3. **Transparency:** AI systems can be complex and opaque, making it difficult for users to understand how decisions are being made. This lack of transparency can erode trust, especially if users feel that the AI is acting in ways that are unpredictable or unfair. Organizations will need to ensure that their AI systems are not only effective but also transparent and explainable.

The Emergence of Quantum Computing

Quantum computing, once the stuff of science fiction, is rapidly approaching reality. Unlike classical computers, which use bits to process information, quantum computers use quantum bits (qubits) that can represent multiple states simultaneously. This allows quantum computers to perform certain calculations exponentially faster than classical computers.

But with great power comes great responsibility—and a new set of ethical challenges:

1. **Cryptography and Security:** Quantum computers have the potential to break current cryptographic systems, rendering much of today's data security infrastructure obsolete. This poses a significant risk to data privacy and security. Organizations will need to explore quantum-resistant encryption methods and prepare for a future where traditional encryption is no longer secure.

2. **Data Integrity:** The speed and complexity of quantum computing could lead to new challenges in ensuring data integrity. Quantum computers might solve problems so quickly that there's little time to verify the accuracy or fairness of the outcomes. Organizations will need to develop new methods for validating quantum-generated results to maintain trust in their systems.

3. **Access and Inequality:** Quantum computing technology is likely to be expensive and require specialized knowledge to operate. This could create a digital divide, where only the most resource-rich organizations can afford to implement quantum computing, leading to inequalities in technological capabilities.

Ensuring equitable access to quantum technology will be an important ethical consideration.

Data Sovereignty and Privacy

As more organizations move to the cloud and globalize their operations, data sovereignty—where data is stored and who has jurisdiction over it—will become a critical issue. Different countries have different laws governing data storage and access, and navigating these regulations can be a legal and ethical minefield.

Consider this: Your organization is storing data in a country with strict privacy laws. Suddenly, a government agency from another country requests access to that data as part of an investigation. What do you do? Comply with the request and potentially violate the local privacy laws, or refuse and risk legal repercussions from the requesting country?

The ethical challenges of data sovereignty require organizations to be proactive in understanding the legal landscape, ensuring that their data storage practices are compliant with all relevant regulations, and being prepared to navigate complex cross-border issues. It's like playing chess on a global scale, but with a lot more at stake than just bragging rights.

Sustainability and Green IT

Sustainability is no longer a "nice-to-have"—it's a must-have. As concerns about climate change and resource scarcity grow, organizations are under increasing pressure to adopt sustainable practices, and ITSM is no exception.

In the future, we can expect to see more organizations embracing Green IT initiatives, such as reducing energy consumption in data centers, minimizing e-waste, and sourcing IT equipment from sustainable suppliers. But sustainability isn't just about protecting the planet; it's also about doing what's right for society and future generations.

The ethical implications of sustainability in ITSM are clear: Organizations have a responsibility to reduce their environmental impact, not just because it's good for business, but because it's the right thing to do. And let's be honest—nobody wants to be remembered as the organization that single-handedly kept a landfill in business.

The Ethical Implications of Remote Work

The rise of remote work has transformed the way we think about ITSM. No longer confined to a physical office, IT services must now support a distributed workforce, often spread across multiple time zones and continents. This shift brings new ethical challenges, from ensuring data security in home office environments to respecting employees' work-life balance.

1. **Data Security:** When employees work from home, the lines between personal and professional data can blur. Organizations need to implement robust security measures to protect sensitive information, while also respecting employees' privacy rights. After all, nobody wants their IT department snooping through their personal cat photos.

2. **Work-Life Balance:** Remote work offers flexibility, but it can also lead to burnout if employees feel pressured to be "always on." Organizations have an ethical responsibility to support employees' well-being by promoting a healthy work-life balance and setting clear boundaries around work hours. Because let's face it—no one's best ideas come at 3 a.m. after their fourth cup of coffee.

3. **Digital Inclusion:** As remote work becomes more prevalent, it's important to ensure that all employees have access to the tools and resources they need to succeed, regardless of their location

or circumstances. This includes providing access to reliable internet, offering training on digital tools, and ensuring that remote work policies are inclusive and equitable.

The Role of Ethics in Emerging Technologies

As new technologies continue to emerge, the ethical landscape of ITSM will become increasingly complex. From blockchain and quantum computing to the Internet of Things (IoT) and 5G, each new technology brings its own set of ethical considerations.

For example, blockchain technology offers enhanced security and transparency, but it also raises questions about privacy and the potential for misuse. Similarly, the widespread adoption of IoT devices could lead to unprecedented levels of data collection, creating new challenges around consent, data ownership, and surveillance.

Organizations will need to stay ahead of the curve by continuously assessing the ethical implications of new technologies and adapting their ITSM practices accordingly. This means not only understanding the technical aspects of these technologies but also considering how they impact users, society, and the environment.

Case Study: Navigating the Future of ITSM with Integrity

Let's consider a global technology company, TechForward, which is integrating AI, blockchain, and IoT into its ITSM practices to stay ahead in the competitive market. The company is committed to leveraging these emerging technologies to improve service delivery, but it also faces significant ethical challenges.

The Dilemma: TechForward's AI-driven analytics platform has the potential to revolutionize IT service delivery by predicting outages and automating responses. However, during testing, the team discovered that the AI algorithms were disproportionately affecting certain user groups, leading to unfair prioritization. At the same time, the company's implementation of IoT devices raised concerns about data privacy, particularly in regions with strict data protection laws.

The Decision: Rather than rushing to deploy the new technologies, TechForward took a step back to reassess its approach. The company decided to pause the rollout of the AI platform to address the bias in the algorithms, ensuring that the system treated all users fairly. Additionally, TechForward worked closely with legal experts to navigate the complex landscape of data privacy laws, implementing robust data protection measures that complied with local regulations.

The Outcome: By prioritizing ethical considerations, TechForward not only avoided potential legal and reputational risks but also gained the trust of its users and stakeholders. The company's decision to address the ethical challenges upfront allowed it to create a more inclusive and transparent ITSM environment, setting a standard for ethical technology use in the industry.

Lessons Learned: TechForward's experience highlights the importance of taking a proactive approach to ethics in ITSM, especially when dealing with emerging technologies. By addressing ethical challenges early and prioritizing fairness, transparency, and compliance, organizations can navigate the future of ITSM with integrity.

Practical Tips for Ethical ITSM in the Future

As we look to the future, here are some practical steps you can take to ensure that your ITSM practices remain ethical and responsible:

1. **Stay Informed:** Keep up to date with the latest developments in technology, ethics, and regulations. This will help you anticipate

potential ethical challenges and adapt your ITSM practices accordingly.

2. **Engage Stakeholders:** Involve a diverse range of stakeholders in decision-making processes, including employees, customers, legal experts, and ethicists. This will help you consider different perspectives and make more informed ethical decisions.

3. **Implement Ethical AI Practices:** If you're using AI in your ITSM processes, ensure that your algorithms are trained on diverse, representative data. Regularly audit your AI systems for bias and take steps to address any issues that arise.

4. **Prioritize Sustainability:** Make sustainability a core part of your ITSM strategy. This includes reducing your environmental impact, sourcing IT equipment from sustainable suppliers, and promoting Green IT practices throughout your organization.

5. **Promote Digital Inclusion:** Ensure that your ITSM practices are inclusive and accessible to all employees, regardless of their location, background, or abilities. This might involve offering additional support or training for remote workers or designing IT services that accommodate a wide range of needs.

6. **Explore Quantum-Resistant Solutions:** As quantum computing advances, begin exploring quantum-resistant encryption methods to ensure your data remains secure in the future. This might involve collaborating with research institutions or investing in early-stage quantum technologies.

7. **Adopt a Precautionary Approach to New Technologies:** Before adopting emerging technologies like blockchain or IoT, conduct thorough ethical assessments to identify potential risks and ensure that your implementation strategies align with your organization's values and ethical standards.

8. **Foster a Culture of Continuous Learning:** Encourage your IT team to continuously develop their skills and knowledge in both technology and ethics. This can involve attending workshops, participating in industry forums, or engaging in cross-disciplinary learning to stay ahead of the curve.

Conclusion: Navigating the Future with Integrity

The future of ITSM is full of possibilities, but it's also fraught with challenges. As technology continues to evolve, so will the ethical considerations that ITSM professionals must navigate. But with the right approach, these challenges can be turned into opportunities to build a more ethical, responsible, and sustainable future for ITSM.

So, what's the key to navigating the future of ITSM with integrity? It's about staying informed, being proactive, and always putting ethics at the forefront of your decision-making process. It's about balancing the benefits of new technologies with their potential risks and ensuring that your IT services are not only effective but also aligned with your organization's values.

In the end, the future of ITSM is in your hands. By embracing ethical principles and leading with integrity, you can help shape a future where technology serves the greater good—where IT services not only support business goals but also contribute to a better world.

And who knows? With a little foresight, a lot of responsibility, and maybe a dash of humor, we can build a future that we're all proud to be a part of.

Appendices

Appendix A: Glossary of Terms

1. **AI (Artificial Intelligence):** The simulation of human intelligence processes by machines, especially computer systems.

2. **Algorithmic Bias:** The presence of systematic and unfair discrimination in the outcomes produced by algorithms or automated decision-making processes. Algorithmic bias can result from biased training data, flawed algorithms, or inappropriate use of data in AI and machine learning systems.

3. **Blockchain:** A decentralized digital ledger that records transactions across many computers in such a way that the registered transactions cannot be altered retroactively, ensuring transparency and security.

4. **Carbon Footprint:** The total amount of greenhouse gases, primarily carbon dioxide (CO_2), emitted directly or indirectly by human activities, such as energy consumption, transportation, and manufacturing. Measuring and reducing the carbon footprint is essential for environmental sustainability.

5. **Cloud Computing:** The delivery of computing services— including servers, storage, databases, networking, software, and analytics—over the internet ("the cloud") to offer faster innovation, flexible resources, and economies of scale.

6. **Code of Ethics:** A set of principles and guidelines that define the ethical standards and expectations for behavior within a particular profession, organization, or community. A code of ethics helps individuals and organizations uphold moral values and conduct.

7. **Compliance:** Adherence to laws, regulations, guidelines, and specifications relevant to the organization's business. In ITSM, compliance often involves ensuring that data management and security practices meet legal and ethical standards.

8. **CSR (Corporate Social Responsibility):** A business model that helps a company be socially accountable to itself, its stakeholders, and the public.

9. **Data Privacy:** The handling of sensitive data, particularly personal data, in a way that respects individual privacy and complies with relevant laws.

10. **Data Sovereignty:** The concept that data is subject to the laws and governance structures within the nation where it is collected. This

is particularly relevant in the context of global cloud computing and data storage.

11. **Deontological Ethics:** An ethical theory that uses rules to distinguish right from wrong.

12. **Digital Ethics:** A branch of ethics that focuses on ethical considerations and principles in the digital realm, including online behavior, data privacy, and the ethical use of technology.

13. **E-Waste:** Discarded electronic appliances such as mobile phones, computers, and televisions.

14. **Ethical AI:** The practice of developing and using artificial intelligence in ways that are fair, transparent, and accountable, ensuring that AI systems do not harm individuals or society.

15. **Ethical Dilemma:** A situation in which a person or organization faces a choice between two or more conflicting ethical principles or values. Ethical dilemmas often require careful consideration and decision-making to determine the most morally appropriate course of action.

16. **GDPR (General Data Protection Regulation):** A regulation in EU law on data protection and privacy in the European Union and the European Economic Area.

17. **Green IT:** Practices that promote environmentally sustainable computing. This includes energy-efficient data centers, sustainable software development, and e-waste management.

18. **Inclusivity:** The practice of actively involving and welcoming individuals from diverse backgrounds, including those of different races, genders, abilities, and cultures. Inclusivity promotes diversity and equal opportunities for all.

19. **IoT (Internet of Things):** The network of physical objects (or "things") that are embedded with sensors, software, and other technologies to connect and exchange data with other devices and systems over the internet.

20. **IT Governance:** The framework that ensures IT investments support business goals. It involves leadership, organizational structures, and processes that ensure that the organization's IT sustains and extends the organization's strategies and objectives.

21. **ITSM (IT Service Management):** The activities that are performed by an organization to design, plan, deliver, operate, and control information technology (IT) services offered to customers.

22. **Least Privilege Principle:** A security concept in which users are granted the minimum levels of access—or permissions—

necessary to perform their job functions. It is a key principle in protecting sensitive data and systems.

23. **Machine Learning:** A subset of AI that involves the use of algorithms and statistical models to enable computers to perform specific tasks without using explicit instructions, relying on patterns and inference instead.

24. **Precautionary Principle:** This principle advises that if an action or policy has the potential to cause harm to the public or the environment, in the absence of scientific consensus, the burden of proof falls on those advocating for the action.

25. **Proportionality Principle:** In security and ethics, this principle states that the measures taken should be proportionate to the risk they are designed to mitigate. This ensures that actions are neither too extreme nor too lenient in addressing potential threats.

26. **Remote Work:** A work arrangement that allows employees to perform their job duties from a location outside the traditional office, often using technology and telecommunication tools to connect with colleagues and access resources.

27. **SaaS (Software as a Service):** A software distribution model in which applications are hosted by a vendor or service provider and

made available to customers over the internet. SaaS eliminates the need for organizations to install and run applications on their own computers.

28. **Stakeholder:** Any individual, group, or entity that has an interest or concern in the activities, decisions, or outcomes of an organization. Stakeholders in ITSM may include customers, employees, suppliers, shareholders, and the community.

29. **Stakeholder Analysis:** The process of identifying and evaluating the interests, needs, and concerns of stakeholders in order to make informed decisions and manage relationships effectively. Stakeholder analysis helps organizations understand the impact of their actions on various stakeholders.

30. **Supply Chain Ethics:** The ethical considerations and practices related to the procurement and management of goods and services within an organization's supply chain. Supply chain ethics address issues such as fair labor practices, environmental responsibility, and responsible sourcing.

31. **Sustainability Reporting:** The practice of disclosing an organization's environmental, social, and governance (ESG) performance and impacts through formal reports and disclosures.

Sustainability reporting provides transparency and accountability regarding sustainability efforts.

32. **Transparency:** The quality of being open, honest, and easily understood in one's actions, decisions, and communication. Transparency is crucial for building trust and demonstrating ethical conduct.

33. **Utilitarianism:** An ethical theory that determines right from wrong by focusing on outcomes. It is a form of consequentialism.

34. **Virtualization:** The process of creating a virtual version of something, such as a server, a storage device, or network resources. Virtualization allows multiple virtual systems to run on a single physical system, improving resource utilization and flexibility.

Appendix B: List of Resources and Further Reading

1. **"ITIL Foundation: ITIL 4 Edition"** by Axelos: A comprehensive guide to the ITIL framework and its applications.

2. **"The Ethics of Information Technology and Business"** by Richard T. De George: This book discusses the ethical issues and challenges in the business use of information technology.

3. **"Data Ethics: The New Competitive Advantage"** by Gry Hasselbalch and Pernille Tranberg: Insights into how businesses can leverage ethical data practices.

4. **"AI Ethics"** by Mark Coeckelbergh: A discussion on the ethical aspects of artificial intelligence and its implications in various sectors.

5. **Online Course: "Ethics in AI and Big Data"** by the Linux Foundation: An exploration of ethical considerations in AI and big data.

Appendix C: About the Author

Naza Semenoff is a seasoned subject matter expert with over two decades of distinguished experience in the world of IT governance, IT Operations, IT Service Management, and best practices. Throughout her illustrious career, she has been a trusted advisor to C-level executives, guiding them through intricate terrains of target operating models, IT strategies, and crucial IT processes, including the nuanced areas of IT onboarding and offboarding.

Having authored two impactful books, "Fit for Service: Navigating the Crossroads of FitSM" and "IT Onboarding and Offboarding," Naza Semenoff is a recognized authority in the field. Her publications are a testament to her commitment to sharing knowledge and expertise with a wider audience.

Operating across diverse industries such as Financial Services, Healthcare, Education, Hospitality, and Technology, Naza has consistently demonstrated an adeptness in identifying, architecting, and implementing optimized solutions. Her insights into technology strategy, transformation, business process optimization, and cybersecurity defenses bear the hallmark of her deep expertise and hands-on approach.

But the author's reputation extends beyond mere strategy and execution. She is known for her proficiency in bridging the traditional divide between business objectives and IT capabilities. With a particular emphasis on IT governance, effectiveness, and alignment with business goals, she has consistently provided direction, ensuring that IT initiatives are both sustainable and beneficial in the long run.

Being a certified ITIL Expert and an OKR Coach, Naza doesn't just rely on theoretical knowledge; she brings to the table tried and tested methodologies, ensuring that organizations reap the rewards of best practices in the realm of organizational capabilities. Her academic pursuits, which include an MBA and an engineering degree, further solidify her position as a thought leader in her domain.

In this book, Naza Semenoff distills her vast reservoir of knowledge, offering readers a glimpse into the expertise that has made her a sought-after consultant and strategist in the IT landscape.

Index

A

- Accountability, 30

- AI (Artificial Intelligence), 5, 27, 79, 91, 93, 98

- Algorithmic Bias, 12, 91

- Automation, 12, 30, 79

B

- Blockchain, 85, 86, 89, 91

C

- Carbon Footprint, 57, 58, 62, 91

- Cloud Computing: 65, 75, 92, 93

- Code of Ethics, 92

- Compliance, 13, 22, 23, 41, 64, 71, 77, 87, 92

- Corporate Social Responsibility (CSR), 61

- CSR's Role in Ethical ITSM, 61, 92

www.ingramcontent.com/pod-product-compliance
Lightning Source LLC
LaVergne TN
LVHW051711050326
832903LV00032B/4131